Self –Publishing 101

Self-Publishing Made Easy

Dr. Ulyses A Pratt III

Self-Publishing 101

Copyright © 2023 by Dr. Ulyses A. Pratt III

ISBN -10 88909902116
ISBN -13 979889090902115
Library of Congress Control Number: 2023919630

Manual Overview

- ✓ What is Self- Publishing
- ✓ Getting Started
- ✓ The Book Outline
- ✓ Understanding the Editing Process
- ✓ The difference between Self –Publishing and a Publishing House.
- ✓ Understanding the ISBN
- ✓ Understanding the Copyright Process
- ✓ Understanding the Library of Congress
- ✓ Tips to Remember

OUR PURPOSE

Our Purpose is to provide you with valuable steps in understanding the process of self publishing, as well as developing a strategy that is measurable.

_____
_____
_____
_____
_____
_____
_____
_____
_____
_____
_____
_____
_____
_____
_____
_____
_____
_____
_____
_____
_____
_____

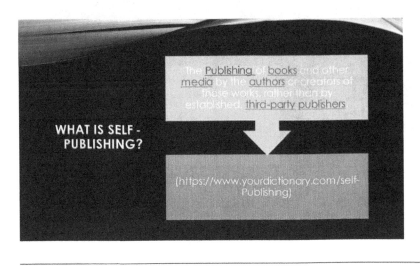

WHAT IS SELF - PUBLISHING?

The _Publishing_ of _books_ and other _media_ by the _authors_ or creators of those works, rather than by established, _third-party publishers_

(https://www.yourdictionary.com/self-Publishing)

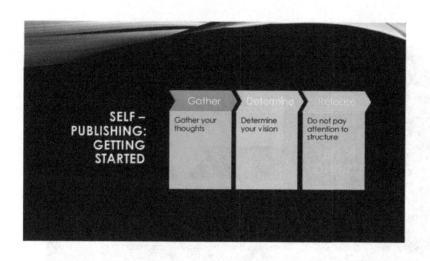

SELF – PUBLISHING: GETTING STARTED

Gather	Determine	Release
Gather your thoughts	Determine your vision	Do not pay attention to structure

GETTING STARTED: CONTINUED

WHO IS MY AUDIENCE?

WHO IS MY TARGET LOCATION?

DO I HAVE A SERIES?

_____
_____
_____
_____
_____
_____
_____
_____
_____
_____
_____
_____
_____
_____
_____
_____
_____
_____

THE BOOK OUTLINE

The Preface	Dedication	Table of Contents
Foreword	Introduction	Acknowledgements

_____
_____
_____
_____
_____
_____
_____
_____
_____
_____
_____
_____
_____
_____
_____
_____
_____
_____
_____

THE BOOK OUTLINE

The Preface

The preface gives you, as the author, the opportunity to introduce yourself to your readers and explain to them why they should hear what you have to say.

The Dedication

The dedication normally is not long. It can be a sentence or two, to honor someone in the life of the author.

_____

_____

_____

_____

_____

_____

_____

_____

_____

_____

_____

_____

_____

_____

_____

_____

THE BOOK OUTLINE

- **The Table of Contents**

A list of divisions (chapters or articles) and the pages on which they start.

The Foreword

The content provided in the foreword should introduce the author or work to readers, tell readers why they should read the book, and give credibility to the book or author.

_____

_____

_____

_____

_____

_____

_____

_____

_____

_____

_____

_____

_____

_____

_____

_____

_____

THE BOOK OUTLINE

The Introduction

The introduction is where you want to explain what your book is about by touching on the major themes.

The Biography

An account of someone's life written by someone else

The Acknowledgement

An **acknowledgement** is a statement of gratitude for assistance in producing a work.

_____

_____

_____

_____

_____

_____

_____

_____

_____

_____

_____

_____

_____

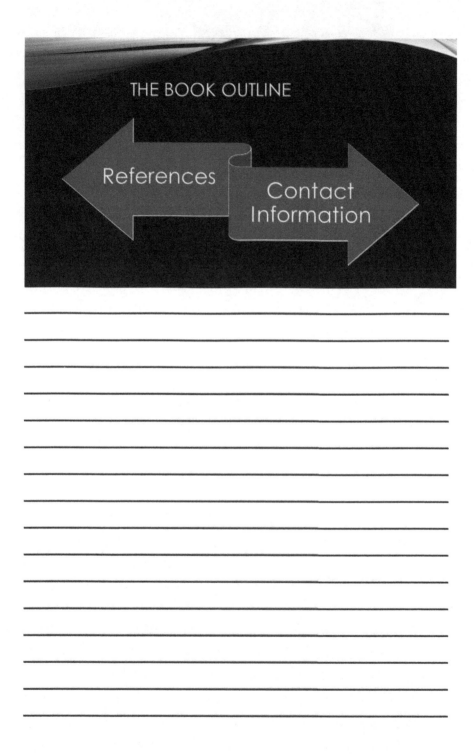

THE BOOK OUTLINE

References   Contact Information

_____
_____
_____
_____
_____
_____
_____
_____
_____
_____
_____
_____
_____
_____
_____
_____
_____

THE EDITING PROCESS

- The editing process can involve correction, condensation, organization, and many other modifications performed with an intention of producing a correct, consistent, accurate and complete work.

EDITING TIPS: TIPS TO CONSIDER

1. Editing a book is different from editing a class paper.
2. Do not write the book in terms of how the person talks.
3. Always have a second set of eyes looking over your manuscript.
4. Pay attention to grammar.
5. Pay attention to the use of words: Example their, there, they're.
6. Pay attention to spelling.

THE ADVANTAGES SELF PUBLISHING

Advantages	Things to Consider
Full ownership of rights and royalties	You must make sure the book is good in all aspects. If it's unprofessional in any way (writing, cover, marketing, etc.), it will make you look bad.
Completely customizable in all aspects	It's time consuming to learn and manage the process yourself.
Fast to market (6 months)	If you hire excellent professionals to help you, it's expensive.
Complete marketing control	Must put the work in
Complete creative control	Must put the work in
Complete freedom, no gatekeepers telling you what you can and cannot do	Must put the work in

_____

_____

_____

_____

_____

_____

_____

_____

_____

_____

_____

_____

_____

_____

_____

_____

THINGS TO CONSIDER IN TERMS OF PUBLISHING COMPANIES

1. Contract.
2. No ownership in terms of manuscript.
3. There are additional fees.

_____
_____
_____
_____
_____
_____
_____
_____
_____
_____
_____
_____
_____
_____
_____
_____
_____

THE PURPOSE OF THE (ISBN)

The International Standard Book Number (ISBN) is a numeric commercial book identifier which is intended to be unique. Publishers purchase ISBNs from an affiliate of the International ISBN Agency.

ISBN 978-0-9557163-0-0

9 780955 716300

THE PURPOSE O THE (ISBN)

- An ISBN improves the likelihood your book will be found and purchased.
- An ISBN links to essential information about your book.
- An ISBN enables more efficient marketing and distribution of your title.
- Most retailers require ISBNs.
- Correct use of the ISBN allows different product forms and editions of a book, printed or digital, to be differentiated clearly, ensuring that customers receive the version they require.
- An ISBN helps you to collect and analyze book sales data.

PURCHASING THE (ISBN)

- https://www.myidentifiers.com

$150 The ISBN is the global standard for identifying titles
- Having a barcode on your book will facilitate automated sales and inventory tracking

PURCHASING THE (ISBN)

- ISBN full distribution registration to Books In Print and U.S. ISBN Agency with full upload of PDF which enhances book search ability in all search engines and full front cover upload for all catalogues in books in print distribution
  - Basic Package
    - $25
- https://www.thebookpatch.com
  - Enhanced Package
    - $40
  - Premium Package
    - $50

THE COPYRIGHT

- https://www.**copyright**.gov
  - Click

  - Registration
    - Click

- Register Your Work: Registration Portal

THE USER LOGIN PROCESS FOR THE COPYRIGHT

User Login

If you are a registered user, please login here.
User ID: *

Password: *

Forgot Your Password or User Id ? / Reset Your Password ?

If you are a new user, click here to register.

Welcome!

Welcome to the Electronic Copyright Office (eCO)

You may now use this website to:

* Register your work

* Preregister your work if you fulfill the requirements

* Submit electronic works to comply with a Notice for Mandatory Deposit

FINISHING THE COPYRIGHT PROCESS

Click New Publication

- Enter in the name of the book
  - Enter the ISBN number:
    - Register you work

- The cost you will pay is $60.00. The copyright certificate will be sent by mail. The status can be checked by logging into your account. Follow this process each time you create a new publication. After you are done, you will have the option to upload you PDF version of your book to the system instead of sending your Manuscript by mail.

THE LIBRARY OF CONGRESS

https://www.loc.gov/publish/pcn/about/index.html

The purpose of the Preassigned Control Number (PCN) Program is to enable the Library of Congress to assign Library of Congress Control Numbers (LCCN) in advance of publication to those titles that may be added to the Library collections. The publisher prints the LCCN in the book and thereby facilitates cataloging and other book processing activities. The PCN links the book to any record which the Library of Congress, other libraries, bibliographic utilities, and book vendors may create.

THE LIBRARY OF CONGRESS

Traditional publishers who would like to participate in the PCN Program must first create an account in PrePub Book Link. Once the publisher account has been approved, publishers can begin submitting LCCN requests. Publishing houses with multiple imprints should create an account for each imprint

Authors and **self-publishers** can submit an LCCN request after creating an account in PrePub Book Link without waiting for approval by Library staff

Based on the information provided by the publisher, Library staff assign a preassigned Library of Congress Control Number (LCCN) to each title. The publisher prints the LCCN on the back of the title page (i.e., the copyright page) in the following manner

Library of Congress Control Number: 201901234

THE LIBRARY OF CONGRESS

Create your Account

* First Name

* Last Name

* Email

* PasswordShow

Create An Account

THE LIBRARY OF CONGRESS

We received your Preassigned Control Number (PCN) request for Example: How To Maximize Your Purpose ISBN 2572545677248.

Please print the text and the Library of Congress control number (LCCN) exactly as it appears below on the copyright page of this book:

Library of Congress Control Number: 2010413584

Please log into your PrePub Book Link account to submit a Change Request if any bibliographic information pertaining to your forthcoming book changes.

Please send a complimentary copy of the best edition of the book immediately upon publication to:

_____

_____

_____

_____

_____

_____

_____

_____

_____

_____

_____

_____

_____

_____

_____

_____

_____

_____

THE LIBRARY OF CONGRESS

Library of Congress
US Programs, Law, and Literature Division
Cataloging in Publication Program
101 Independence Avenue, S.E.
Washington, DC 20540-4283

_____

_____

_____

_____

_____

_____

_____

_____

_____

_____

_____

_____

_____

_____

_____

_____

_____

_____

_____

Quick Price:

$213.50

Price/Book:

$4.27/book

50 Books

Rush Services:

- Standard (Ships in 2 day(s)*) + $0.00
- Rush (Ships in 1 day*) + $32.03
- Super Rush (Ships same day*) + $74.72

TIPS TO REMEMBER

1. Marketing
2. Book cover
3. Formatting
4. Website
5. Photography
6. eBook
7. Cost
8. Amazon
9. Book Signing

_____
_____
_____
_____
_____
_____
_____
_____
_____
_____
_____
_____
_____
_____
_____
_____
_____

REFERENCES

- https://www.**isbn.org**
- j wr u‹lly y y 0j gdqqm c\ej Œqo
- www.48hourbooks.com
- https://kdp.amazon.com
- US Copyright Office - Official Site
- https://www.**copyright**.gov

https://www.loc.gov/publish/pcn/about/index.html

About the Author

Mr. Ulyses A. Pratt III was born to Peggy Glass and Ulyses Pratt JR. on April 6, 1979. He graduated University City High School in 1998. He is a graduate from Eastern University with a

Bachelor of Arts Degree in Organizational Leadership. In 2007, he received an opportunity to study abroad with students from Eastern University to travel to Cairo Egypt. In 2008 he received his Diploma in Ministerial Leadership from the School of the Word Bible Institute from Victory Christian Center in Philadelphia, PA where he is also licensed as a Deacon. In 2009, he received the opportunity to serve as a camp counselor for Laurel Mountain Christian Camp in Rector PA, where he worked with inner city youth from Pittsburgh.

He also volunteered as a mentor for the People for People Mentoring Children of Purpose program. This program provides mentorship to children ages 4-18, who have at least one parent that is incarcerated.

In 2010, Mr. Pratt became the Founder and CEO of Ulyses Pratt Enterprises, LLC, a Limited Liability Corporation that is geared toward promoting empowerment, spiritual growth, and professional development seminars for the community. The mission of this organization is to "Transform Lives Through Empowerment." This business has allowed Mr. Pratt to host two successful seminars entitled How To Release Your Potential and Becoming a Strategic Leader for the next Generation. Within the same year, Mr. Pratt became the author of his first book entitled "It's Not Your Fault: A Guide to Overcoming Strongholds," and he was ordained into the Office of a Deacon.

In 2012 Mr. Pratt wrote his second book "entitled Dreaming Big for Life: How to make your Dreams for you, Volume 1. In 2013 Mr. Pratt became the founder and CEO of his non-profit organization called Helping People International. This organization's primary focus is to empower and develop the community abroad.

In 2014 Mr. Pratt was blessed to be joined together to the love of his life, Chanika Pratt. In 2015 Mr. Pratt Graduated from Walden University with his Master's Degree in Leadership Development.

In that same year, Mr. Pratt became a licensed Minster by Victory Christian Center of Philadelphia, Pa where the pastor and founder is Apostle Dr. Jimmie A. Elis III. Mr. and Mrs. Pratt were blessed in that same year with their beautiful daughter Analee Marie Pratt.

Mr. Pratt has been ordained an Elder in 2019 from Victory Christian of Philadelphia. Mr. Pratt is the author of eight published books.

In Mr. 2020 Mr. Pratt received his Doctor of Ministry Degree from Destiny Theological Institute and Seminary. In 2021 Mr. Pratt was ordained as Pastor, in that same year become the Founder of the Lighthouse Church International. Mr. Pratt and Mrs. Pratt are the Pastors of this great fellowship. Mr. Pratt is thankful to God for all the things that He has done, not to mention the prayers and the support of His mother Deaconess Peggy Glass.